C0-GCJ-160

WE LIVE TO LOVE, TO HOPE, AND TO LAUGH

THROUGH ART AND WORDS OF EXPRESSION

by

Robin Charnel Blackmon

DORRANCE
PUBLISHING CO
EST. 1920
PITTSBURGH, PENNSYLVANIA 15238

The contents of this work, including, but not limited to, the accuracy of events, people, and places depicted; opinions expressed; permission to use previously published materials included; and any advice given or actions advocated are solely the responsibility of the author, who assumes all liability for said work and indemnifies the publisher against any claims stemming from publication of the work.

All Rights Reserved
Copyright © 2021 by Robin Charnel Blackmon

No part of this book may be reproduced or transmitted, downloaded, distributed, reverse engineered, or stored in or introduced into any information storage and retrieval system, in any form or by any means, including photocopying and recording, whether electronic or mechanical, now known or hereinafter invented without permission in writing from the publisher.

Dorrance Publishing Co
585 Alpha Drive
Pittsburgh, PA 15238
Visit our website at *www.dorrancebookstore.com*

ISBN: 978-1-6491-3838-5
eISBN: 978-1-6491-3999-3

WELCOME

Thank you for taking the time to read *We Live to Love, Hope, and Laugh: Through Art and Words of Expression* inspired by the beauty of the emotional power of artwork. We are born with the gift of imagination produced by a Creator who is unlimited in creation beyond our imagination.

I hope this book will bring you comfort, encouragement, inspiration, peace, and hope during trials. Be blessed as you embrace the power of love.

Thank you,
Robin C. Blackmon

DEDICATION

As a mother, my children have taught me through my commitment to them to be responsible, to learn to live in the moment, and put my best foot forward.

Jaida, my firstborn, whose spirit is magnetic to those she meets, thank you for teaching me affection and being my support system throughout each endeavor.

Aaron, my second born, a leader who gives effortlessly, thank you for always making sure your mother and siblings are good.

Elijah, my third born, blessed with a heart that cares for the less fortunate, thank you for being so caring and teaching us to, "pray without ceasing" (1 Thess 5:17).

As a daughter raised by a strong woman in faith, she prayed for me to be meek and humble. Overshadowed by growing up in a rough neighborhood in San Francisco, my mother would refer to me as a diamond in the rough. My mother Cynthia L. Blackmon has always been an encouraging source of love in my life. Thank you, Mother, for giving me your best.

As a daughter raised by a kind father in faith, my father's prayers remain for me to be safe. My father Robert L. Seymore blessed me with the gift of unconditional love and changed my life completely. His heart overflows with the gift of giving, laughter, and protection. Thank you, Dad, for always making me feel loved and giving me your all.

As a little sister, my brothers taught me street smarts, observation, and to think quickly. Thank you for spoiling me and being overprotective, for it worked out for my good. I love you.

As an aunt, I feel blessed to have a trustworthy relationship with my nieces and nephews. Thank you for allowing me to be a part of your world.

As a friend, I am grateful to have the same childhood friends in my adulthood. Thank you, lovely women, for being so amazing and inspiring. I thank God for you all.

As a potential wife, thank you to the man who reminded me I am created to love. Thank you for not giving up on me.

To my gifted friend, Jennifer King, thank you for the best birthday gift I received in 2019. An original J. L. King painting; how I see myself sparked a light of words from within. Thank you to the three lovely women who encouraged this book to come to life, to Cynthia Blackmon, NeKeisha Ray, and Rita Sabini.

Mother, thank you for always expressing when the writings spoke to your heart. You continue to point out the gifts from God that you see within. Thank you for being an encourager.

NeKeisha, thank you for being my cheerleader and sounding board. You challenged me to strive. Especially when I felt this project would be impossible to complete, you continuously put me back together. With each writing, you cheered me on, reminding me God is infinite.

Rita, thank you for your insight, feedback, encouraging words, and for expressing how you foresee sermons coming forth and the gift to minister God's word.

I love you all,
Robin C. Blackmon

CONTENTS

FORT FUNSTON BEACH

MARINA GREEN

Images by Robin C. Blackmon

ACKNOWLEDGMENTS

I dedicate this book to my Heavenly Father. Lord, You have been extremely kind and patient with me. You bless Your children daily with the gift of expression, creativity, love, and awareness of who you are.

I thank You for allowing me to fall back in love with writing. Thank You for touching J. L. King's heart to paint the beautiful picture of the woman who is a reflection of women who have come before me, walk with me, and who will come after me. J. L. King's vision was the trigger to ignite the gift You placed in me so long ago.

You are the Creator of all things, and I thank You for the gift of Your Holy Spirit to allow me the words of expression.

To my grandparents, uncles, and aunties thank you, for being men of integrity, women of grace, and devoted to the word of God.

The gifts I have received passed down from generation to generation, keep me in awe and in love with our Father every day. I truly understand your work here on earth.

Tonisha, thank you for your everlasting support. Thank you for your prayer over me after my graduation. You continuously inspire and encourage those surrounded by your love and gift of discernment. Thank you for being my rock, protector, and prayer warrior.

With Love,
Robin C. Blackmon

INTRODUCTION

I remember as a teen, Hallmark cards and love songs moved me. Words have always impressed me. Not just any words, but words of expression. I did not realize how effective I was with words until my late girlfriend Tamika LaDawn Mack would encourage me to help write love letters. I have always believed in the power of words, but not enough to share my thoughts with the world until I enrolled in Bible Base Ministry School of Theology.

I recall having a conversation my first semester with my mentor, who also was my uncle, Pastor Larry Mitchell, nickname Doc. Others will say he was a living encyclopedia for the word of God. I expressed to him how I enjoy writing and wanted to write about the woman "which had a spirit of infirmity eighteen years." (Luke 13:1) He was thrilled as he encouraged me to do so. His exact words were, "I am excited to read what the Holy Spirit will reveal to you." Sadly that day never came. My uncle passed away from cancer 17 hours before receiving the news I would be participating in the 2018 graduation to receive my bachelor's degree in Biblical Studies. That moment made history. I graduated with my aunt, Dr. Alta Faye Regan. My aunt received her doctorate that day. I received the joy of the Spirit and the honor of becoming the third generation in ministry.

I dedicate these writings, which project the Spirit of God, to my late Uncle Pastor Larry Mitchell. May the words from my heart be lifted. May he be smiling from above, singing words of assurance to me. "Yes, niece you got it."

SECTION 1

HE LIVES

Come unto me, all ye that labour and are heavy laden, and I will give you rest.

Take my yoke upon you and learn of me; for I am meek and lowly in heart and ye shall find rest unto your souls.

For my yoke is easy, and my burden is light.

– Matthew 11:28-30 (KJV)

Image by Jeff Jacobs from Pixabay

GOD'S GIFT

To receive God's gift of life is to breathe the fullness of His breath;
The air becomes fuel to the body to create a natural resource of energy and power.
Inhale, exhale to the rhythm of His heart, for every breath is borrowed;
His fullness has no limitation, for the whistling wind is how His Spirit flows
and moves throughout the mist of the air.
To encounter the wind is to embrace the melody of sound brushing against your ear;
The octave wind has no set level to the frequency of vibration, for He is omnipotent.
As the wind whispers to water in command to move with exceeding heights
inconceivable to fathom,
He is the slight breeze which gives life to each ripple; as He walks upon the waters,
The stillness of the gentle breeze is peace within the realm of His horizons.
God reveals his infinite love as we partake in the fullness of the air we breathe, for
He giveth life (Genesis 1:2 KJV).

Images by Robin C. Blackmon

UNWAVERING LOVE

What is unwavering love?
Unwavering love is a commitment that does not seek any other alternative nor solution;
To willfully endure the profundity of the process, to fulfill the promise of eternal life made in love.
Unwavering love is patient in understanding, as forbearing is contentment in longsuffering,
Which measures to abundant love;
Unwavering love is obedience unto death.
He unselfishly yielded to the sacrificial course of events; He conquered death in love.
Unwavering love does not surrender to circumstance or succumb to the mocking and trial but depends upon the Spirit's divine love of forgiveness;
He intercedes, "Father forgive them for they know not what they do."
Unwavering love is the blood that flows from heaven to Earth with the power to heal and to wash the repentant sin away. Atonement; sin was defeated upon the cross.
Unwavering love is the rising of the sun, for His breath is a reminder; His mercies are afresh with each morning.
Unwavering love is the gift of grace to the unworthy,
For we are sinners saved by grace.
Unwavering love is salvation at the cross the moment
Christ gave up the Ghost.
John 3:16 Mark 15:37 Luke 23:34

Image by David Mark from Pixabay

VIRTUOUS

To behold God's daughter is to witness her heart,
For her heart is the utmost source of why she thrives;
Her heart is the core of her existence.
Created by love, to love, her heart is what makes her gracefully divine.
The essence of her beauty cannot be defined, for the magnitude of her selflessness is the reflection of her beauty.
She loves deeply; her love for God's children flows immeasurable, deep like an ocean.
Her obedience to God unveils unconditional love, which organically feeds peace and harmony to a nation.
Meekness is what she desires, for she understands, it is God who called her by name.
Humble child, for her acts in humility showcase evidence of her prayers;
Her commitment to loyalty and dedication sits upon her shoulders, yet she does not crumble,
Set free of all past hurt and pain; her wounds exude a majestic fragrance of a delicate flower.
She takes pride in the washing of her feet, for the soak cleanses away the day's journey.
In her silence, she patiently waits for her strength to be renewed; her fragile heart to be mended by her
Keeper; the winds and storms to pass, for her soul is anchored in contentment.
Her name is virtuous,
Modesty is her gift,
Radiant the world shall see—
She is me.

Image by J.L.King, www.JLKingArt.com

SPIRITUAL METAMORPHOSIS

As I surrender my life to God, my mind and body no longer have the urge to wrestle;
The buckling of my knees brings me to a humble state of submission and honor.
Effortlessly my arms lift toward heaven, as my heart begins to open up;
In the stillness, you hear the beating of my heart synchronize with the whistling wind, as the gentle breeze confirms my heart is ready to yield to the process of transformation.
Encircled by the majestic butterflies, my spirit releases the aroma of sweet nectar that signifies metamorphosis shall begin.
As I succumb to the supernatural state of being, I feel a fresh anointing of pure love fall upon me like the morning dew;
Transformation arises within as I hunger and feast upon the bread of life that slowly feeds nourishment to my soul.
You hide me in an encased protective covering while you renew my mind, transform my body, and the fullness of your attributes are woven within my heart.
I am gracefully broken to be set free, wrapped in the arms of majesty, and transfigured, given wings with the strength of an eagle created to soar.
Matthew 17:2 Ezekiel 36:26 Roman 12:2

Image by Cynthia L. Mitchell

A MOTHER'S LOVE

When left standing with the responsibility to execute the duties of a woman and man,
You must learn to willingly conform to life's sequence of events the best way you can.
A mother's love does not back down at the first sight of life's circumstance;
She dives into the overflow of her trust in God that He knows the outcome beforehand.
When left to carry the torch without a second set of supportive hands,
My arms and the torch did not collapse.
God lifted the weight of my burdens as He held me in the center of his hand,
For a mother's love finds strength in the only one she can depend upon.
When left to raise my voice to mimic the authoritative tone of a man,
The octave without baritone delivered no fear when raising a boy to be a man,
For God created a mother's voice to nurture with love and care.
When left to provide for children while dividing one stipend towards many bills,
You witness the sacrifice is always a blessing in the end,
For God delights in the pure in heart and clean working hands.
When left to work with the strength and the endurance of a man
I learn to receive the Spirit inward pressing as the world witnessed outward drive of perseverance throughout the days' end,
For a Mother's love is a blessing that emanates from within.
When left to raise children until the age of accountability,
You must learn to trust God's process and timing,
For we are God's children, and He has the whole world in His hands.

Images by Tara Russell

SECTION 2

LOVE

When the beauty of your soul kisses your heart, you will know true love.

Its bliss and unconditional sweetness will leave you forever changed.

– Judy Secore

Image by Виктория Бородинова from Pixabay

FOG

What hides behind the somber face of the fog that I cannot discern?
A blurry vision, I yearn to understand clearly,
How do I decipher what I am unable to grasp?
Concealed but capable of being discovered,
Distance in space, yet close enough to feel your existence.
Distorted to others, uniquely created for me.
Fascinated by the perfection of your stature.
Allured by your transparency, I seek to learn the language you speak.
Captivated by the imperfection of your light
The overcast overshadows, the best quality in you;
The cry in you; spark enough light to illuminate through the darkness.
I feel the dew from your tears fall upon my skin,
The agony of brokenness echo in the distance,
Eagerly waiting the moment for the light to shine within thee.
In the wilderness, our souls connect, for light shines in the dark;
We are opposites drawn together by force of nature stimulated by a magnetic impulse, one made exclusively for the other.
My soul feels a faint whisper; rescue me,
For I have no fear of murky conditions.
Conditions have antidotes created with the power to heal,
Hallucination or real, for this level of impact, has no name.
A hidden treasure you are to me; light with no worries I am to you.
What are we?

Image by Robin C. Blackmon

PERFECT LOVE

Can imperfect people produce perfect love,
For our imperfection pushes us toward changes that will make us great.
Our flaws are the hiccups that reveal the authentic parts of which we are:
imperfect human beings experiencing growth through the natural occurrences that keep us grounded.
Our issues do not become a burden that fluctuates the measure of our love.
The errors of our ways become a humbling lesson that teaches us not to judge;
instead patiently communicate with the specks in each other's eyes, for we are like puzzle pieces broken as God's glue mends our brokenness as one.
The tattoo of our identity reads unique, which speaks our truth;
We yield to the unconditional love, a natural complete surrender of, I do.
We are grateful love is not a curious arousal driven by an emotional high,
But an ordained frequency that searches the heart of you and I.
We value love, a yes and a no that can coexist in agreement with no conditions or account to dismiss;
We share a binding force of love simply sealed with a kiss.

Image by Susan Cipriano from Pixabay

LOVES EXPRESSION

Silence is golden when two souls speak with no utterance, just two hearts pulsating simultaneously;
Each breath is the adlib that validates our existence.
The conscious mind needs no words,
For our body language articulates affection to ease the subconscious mind.
Safe in your arms, the gentle touch of your warm embrace generates a satisfaction that confirms, here is where I belong.
Our recipe of elements that form positive energy activates our chemistry, sparking high levels of heat that emits rays of love;
Our foundation sustains the structure that keeps our union solid as we continuously build layers of substantial devotion
Equally filled with the quality of substance; the reflection of our standards show proof that our love needs no words. Love acts out what it feels,
For our love expression will not go unnoticed.
I enjoy loving you.

Image by H.S.Wajid Hussain from Pixabay

PROTOTYPE

The complexity of your prototype comes with a caution.
You are an adventuresome piece to learn, for the detail of your precise work is delicate and fiercely made.
The versatility of your genre makes it challenging to memorize your melody;
Overwhelmed by touch, as I strum, each string vibrates an intricate note that invades my heart.
I become the sounding board, as the base of your body presses into my bosom, transmitting melody that makes my soul sing,
Mesmerized in a trance by your inviting tone, for your ballad falls mute upon the wrong ear;
Audible to the ear that desires to hear the steady cadence of the harmony projected from your heart.
As the sound waves sing our unspoken words, complete, I feel as we intertwine becoming one note, elevating to higher heights;
Our harmony is a significant piece to the chorus of our love.
You are my instrument of choice.

Image by Pexels from Pixabay

WINDOWS TO THE SOUL

We have a natural connection anointed by a superpower energy source that only
two inseparable souls can feel.
Hidden souls exposed at first sight, for our eyes speak a nonverbal language that
collides with intellect.
Enrapture while in penetrating gaze, we recognize the other half of our soul through
the window of our eyes.
The flicker of light in your eyes transmits a glare that adheres to the light deep
within my soul.
My soul can feel the magnitude of your love burst through the windows of your eyes
as they reflect the love you see in me;
Our eyes do not lie, for this level of connection has no guile, no motive, just smitten
by an inward peace driven by affection and security.
Your eyes smile with glee as you watch my soul dance in response to how you look at me.
With a clear vision, you open your heart to collaborate and help heal the worst
part of me.
Within the same breath, you bring out the best in me.
We are each other's equal, for our souls were destined to connect, for we relate to
one another's strength, fears, hopes, and dreams.
As I stare into your eyes, the window to your soul, you are the other half of my soul
that completes me.

Image by Rene Rauschenberger from Pixabay

SECTION 3

OVERCOME TRIALS

God always has something for you, a key for every problem, a light for every shadow, a relief for every sorrow and a plan for every tomorrow.

– Author Unknown

Image by Gerd Altmann from Pixabay

SUN RAYS

The rays from the sun slowly canvas the day's journey,
Beginning with a thorough examination of the heart, mind, and soul.
While the shifting exposes the scattered clouds underlying motives to the merciful
one's eye to read,
Vulnerability attempts to run and hide behind the clouds in hopes to avoid weakness,
Shame no longer wants to wear the cloak of pity,
Acknowledgment fears approaching the light and truth,
Insecurity prays for the wind to blow the lies away,
Accountability pleads with guilt to seek forgiveness towards the light,
Pain desires no recollection in hope for the weather to change.
While the atmosphere orchestrates a multitude of compassion and love within the air,
The soul hungers for righteousness to withstand the force of lies,
The sun rays gleam with endurance and patience to activate the mind to overcome,
The climate produces a massive deliverance to permeate the heart,
Intercession releases the power to peel off unbelief.
Every burden uplifted, weightless with no worry, while you bask in the afterglow of favor;
Forgiveness projects a clean heart if you will just walk into the light.
"I am the light of the world" John 8:12 KJV.

Image by Robin C. Blackmon

PAST HURT

The residue of the past let down has become my worst enemy;
Crippled, off-balanced, for my mind and feet can no longer agree.
Troubled within the deepest level of REM sleep my eyes in rapid movement, for the boogie man keeps chasing me,
Taunting me with words that spell out I don't have a destiny.
As he continues to remind me of past failure, lowering my self-esteem,
No sense of hope to survive this dream, for this beast is strong, and his words keep me in captivity.
Hesitant, is who I have become, for I no longer trust my own capabilities;
To make the right decision will take some form of faith and belief,
But how I can I trust my own judgment based on my past failures and deficiencies?
In no wise can I cry out, although this pain is killing me;
My soul wants to die, but the Spirit says, do not give up on me:
Hope in thy word, and there you will find me.
I have not given you a spirit of fear, but a spirit that depends solely on me
To direct your path, so you may walk into your destiny (Psalm 119:114; Micah 7:8).

Image by JuiMagicman from Pixabay

TRUST THE UNKNOWN

To walk the unknown path towards destiny will take courage to allow the Teacher
to be the way.
Will you surrender to the voice who implanted a vision revealed humanly impossible
to man, yet made possible for the soul that seeks it?
Are you willing to leave behind the only form of comfort you know
To stand on the narrow path with no options of a right or left turn?
Will you accept interference will come with the sense of the journey of location and space,
To press forward against the heavy wind, for the wind does not come to blow you off
course, yet to keep you awake
While the wire will rotate in response to each step, allowing hesitation to give life
to fear of a fall.
Will you trust the Teacher to be the wire, to take solace in? A stumble is not a fall.
Will you believe there is power in the staff you carry, for it provides a balance which
keeps you upright and stable.
For God predestines, He equips, and He qualifies you, for the journey belongs to Him
Will you take the step? (Jeremiah 29:11 NIV/KJV)

Image by Cynthia L. Mitchell

REDEMPTION

Would you be able to cope if you stood behind the windows of my eyes?
Convicted to life in darkness without parole within the cell block of my mind,
With no recourse to loosen the shackles of my thoughts;
Accustomed to darkness, chained to being an outlaw,
My addiction to past emotional hurt and pain allows anger and rejection to be my reason for my sinful acts.
Imprisoned in an internal flame, for my eyes have witnessed the destruction caused by my guilty hands;
Smoking mirrors I represent, for no truth lives in me, just anxiety and hollowness take up residency
While Me, Myself, and I remain in conflict, for we all want to be heard.
If I could strangle Myself, then Me would have the last word,
For Me has allowed Myself and I to run rampant and astray for too long.
A weary soul with no rest; past visions of chaos within my mind bring forth distress
While the inner voice says, "I am here, let me help you past this test."
Repentance is the answer for your soul to receive rest;
Forgiveness is God's gift through the healing process.
If you confess with your tongue, God will give you what is best:
Redemption.

Image by Cocoparisienne from Pixabay

THE KEY

Mentally paralyzed with the inability to turn the key to unlock the door to destiny,
Daily, subconsciously, I travel the same route, overlook the same door that preserves
the answer to my identity.
As I tiptoe around the signs and arrows to avoid God's plan for me,
Comfortably I stagger in darkness given birth to defeat
While the lethal injection of fear in my mind continues to seep excuses to why this
door will not open unto me.
In the midst, the Almighty voice inside affirms, "You hold the key."
My lack of belief is the main course that feeds my insecurities;
The record player in my mind grows weary from harping the same tune stuck on repeat.
The effect of the dull needle causes the record to skip a beat, dwelling on a specific
lyric that reflects the seed sown within me,
While the radiance of life illuminates through the door every second, minute,
an hour, of the day.
I can hear the Almighty voice say, "An abundant life awaits
If you will just turn the key."

Image by WikiImages from Pixabay

SECTION 4

THOUGHTS

The time is always right to do what is right.

—Martin Luther King Jr.

Darkness cannot drive out darkness; only light can do that. Hate cannot drive out hate; only love can do that.

—Martin Luther King Jr.

Image Jackie Ramirez from PixabayImage WikiImages from Pixabay

Photograph taken by Cecil Stoughton July 2,1964, Image WikiImages from Pixabay

WHY DO WE

Why do we anchor resentment in our heart
When God says He will remember our sins no more?
For the deed of a forgiving heart is to uproot and diminish the source of the pain in exchange for peace.
Why do we choose to take hold of the emotion of anxiety and worry about the unknown mysteries of tomorrow
When God said he will supply our every need?
For the works of the Provider are living proof that He is capable of doing so, exceedingly.
Why do we inflict injury to the soul of our neighbor with lethal, unreserved words from our tongue
When God says, "Pleasant words are like a honeycomb, sweet to the soul"?
For operating in kindness will break down the destructive heart.
Why do we live to complain about our troubles
When God gives us grace and sweet mercy, which is sufficient for the day?
For the action of praise displays honor towards the Life-Giver.
Why do we volunteer to wear the scarlet robe and slam a gavel
When God sends rain on the just and unjust?
For the act of passing judgment will only lead to your own judgment (Matthew 5:44-45).

Image by Jackie Ramirez from Pixabay

ARE WE A PEOPLE?

Are we a people who have become desensitized to the needs of the less fortunate?

Are we a people who have become mesmerized by the intentional enhancement of altering deceit?

Are we a people who have become inhumane, put on a deaf ear to the cry of the voices in need?

Are we a people who have become covetous, only gravitate towards the voices who boast loudly about their lavish materialistic things?

Are we a people who have become soulless? We create a sense of blurred vision to avoid the signs that say, "Hungry, please feed me."

Are we a people who have become vain, only have eyes to watch and broadcast our lives on social media and network reality TV?

Are we a people who have become so callous, we cringe with disgust when asked to be a helping hand?

Are we a people who have become haughty, frown upon the lowly in heart rather than give an uplifting smile and extend our hand?

Are we a people who have become uncharitable, ignore the true meaning of kindness?

Are we a people who have become content with forgetting God's commandment, "Thou shalt love thy neighbour as thyself"? (Matt: 22:39)

Image by reneecporter from Pixabay

LIVING IN A TIME

Are we living in a time when wrong is made right and right is no longer normal?
Awkward gestures towards others have no questionable motives;
Children talk over their parents with expression of undeveloped thoughts of shallow concerns; their thoughts reveal their immature senseless lack of logic.
Have parents become too lenient to enforce the boundaries between parent and child, to plant the seeds of obedience, order, and structure, in hope that the child will sprout good character of a decent human being?
Have we become the phrase, "That is not my concern," so we sit back and let a righteous population die?
For senseless logic without reason leads to the destruction of a people.
How do we as a people uphold right from wrong, which makes right dominate, not equate right and wrong?
For wrong is a toxic thought of words formulated by the root of evil acted out by a selfish motive, which causes our nation to crumble.
How do we as a people reclaim prayer back in our schools, to implement prayer on the job, and establish prayer in our homes to overcome the madness of wrong?
For in prayer, we learn to "seek ye first the kingdom of God and his righteousness a nd all these things shall be added unto you." Matthew 6:33 (KJV)

Image by Instagram cdd20 from Pixabay

EARTHLY FATHERLESS CHILDREN

Reproduction is the result of human fertilization, which involves the interweaving of two;
Childbirth is labor and delivery, humanly possible for one, yet an occasion shared by the support of two.
A child has 46 chromosomes, 23 received from each parent, can only be produced by two,
Yet, a single parent lives with the appearance of artificial insemination left to do the job entrusted for two
While the child grows up on an identity quest in search of clues, beginning with traces of DNA that prove, I belong to you.
Agitated by my reflection in the mirror that projects I look like you, mad at the world because I don't even know you;
Crushed with the void of emptiness on the other half of my heart caused by you;
Wounded by the rejection of your lack of phone calls and communication. Where are you?
My behavior shows signs of abandonment, resentment, struggles, and depression.
How my heart cries for you!
If only you could reveal to my ache and pain, what did I do to you
To make you leave me with only imprints of inherited traits? How could you?
Yet, I am created for a purpose by God's grace; I will overcome the absence of you,
By allowing my Heavenly Father to heal my broken wounds.
His grace shows me every day, I am His child, and His compassion is enough to forgive you.
I forgive you, too,
For it all began with two.

Image by Cynthia L. Mitchell

SOULLESS BODY

Do we settle for a body to try to fill voids, so we can feel wanted and not alone?
They say an empty bed is a cold bed when you have no one to share it with,
Yet to share a bed with a body without a soul is even colder.
A soulless body is an empty vessel; it has no heart to love you.
The soulless body is the time filler or parasite that feeds its needs and leaves
 you malnourished;
A soulless body is only a desire that creates an illusion of a right now fix.
The soulless body will verbally create an unrealistic dream
While in the background slips away your self-esteem.
The soulless body could care less about the trials you endure throughout the day;
The soulless body is not attentive to the sadness in your eyes to ask if you are okay.
Overlooks the yearning when all you need is a kiss goodbye,
The soulless body is unavailable, unattainable, and cold as ice.
Its mission on Earth is to be a body without a soul in disguise.
Why do we settle just to have a body in our life?

Image by Efes Kitap from Pixabay

SECTION 5

FUN & CLEVER

I have seen what a laugh can do. It can transform almost unbearable tears into something bearable, even hopeful.

– Bob Hope

Image by Alexas_Fotos from Pixabay

MISSION IMPOSSIBLE

To accomplish the mission impossible to steal your heart will be,
To boldly trigger the invisible laser beam that keeps your heart unattainable to me,
To be prepared to battle the opponents that create a false sense of security,
To dismantle the functioning in self-sabotage and disbelief,
To erase the dysfunctional thoughts created by past pain; still holding onto, "Why me?"
To reason with the voice that questions, "How can she purely love me?"
To eliminate the appetite that keeps you from the joy of monogamy,
To diminish concern and worry that will not allow you to sleep,
To escape mental imprisonment, for you are free indeed.
To remodel the inward infrastructure, weakened by instability,
To terminate heartache and chaos, for your heart hungers for peace.
To implant new methods of survival; learn how to pray with me,
To speak life and discipline in the man you are destined to be,
To witness love in your eyes every time you look at me,
To be the one your heart chooses with every gentle beat,
To tell self-sabotage and disbelief, "You can now be released,"
For the code of conduct is: You do love me.

Image by Jaida Blackmon-Jones

HE IS NOT WHAT I ORDERED

Mesmerized by the suave introduction of your features,
Delusional to the representation of your broken image,
Eager to satisfy the craving within; curiosity willfully overlooks the unhealthy signs.
Avid thirst avoids the small print that states:
"Caution, consumption will impair judgment."
Warned not to let the smooth taste fool me,
I drink from the tall glass of inconsistency as the foam gases me up;
With each sip, I grasp and filter through chosen words to feed my fancy,
Foolishly enamored with the generic taste of your lies, empty promises of
"I will do better," yet your tap runs dry.
The chemical reaction from your synthetic potion has a short- yet long-term
effect of hypnosis;
Deception wears off while the scales over the eyes last a bit longer.
Beware, this type of hangover will leave the mind with the residue of
disappointment and bitterness.
As the artificial flavor dissipates, my taste buds awaken to the foul taste of your
fermentation process that leaves me wanting no more.
He is not what I ordered.

Image by Alexas_Fotos from Pixabay

HOW DO YOU

How do you say good before bye when the heart feels inadequate after you leave?
How does the mind console the heart when the heart shatters from a broken dream?
How do you erase the love shared in each moment when it was love that formed
each memory?
How do you let go of the fantasy of love when the main characters were you and me?
How do you pretend love never existed when we built the bond effortlessly?
How do you accept love lost when the heart desires eternity?
How do you find contentment in the word freedom when the heart does not
want to be free?
How can the heart go on when the heart still believes there is no you without me?

Image by 5593147 by Pixabay

HE IS WHAT I ORDERED

A pleasure to make your acquaintance, for
I have never indulged the smooth taste of your brand.
An acquired taste, you are; the sweet aroma of your malt is tantalizing
Foreign to your attentiveness, as I feel like we're the only two in the room,
Brewing in the thought you speak words of intellect and transparency that ignites
my inner core
While the lyrics of your story remind me of me.
Your special blend of concoction has the ability to quench my thirst.
Refreshing, you are; organically infused with no preservatives nor additives, just the
mixture of exquisite taste.
The authenticity of your best quality makes you top shelf,
Leaving me with butterflies in the hope that we will meet again.
He's exactly what I ordered

Image by Free-Photos from Pixabay

WHEN LOVE IS...

When love is worth the fight,
When love is worth the wait,
We let down our guard to stop playing emotional games.
When love is inescapable,
When love is a fate,
We accept this love is inevitable; we both can't walk away.
When love is attentive,
When love is affectionate,
We cultivate the love that forms our relevance.
When love is a test,
When love is pain,
We learn to humble ourselves; it takes two to stand the rain.
When love is simplistic,
When love is complex,
We expose our vulnerability to keep our insecurity in check.
When love is a risk,
When love is a sure thing,
It's time we gamble on love and commit with two rings...
Will you marry me?

Image by 849356 from Pixabay

ARTIST ACKNOWLEDGMENT WITH GRATITUDE